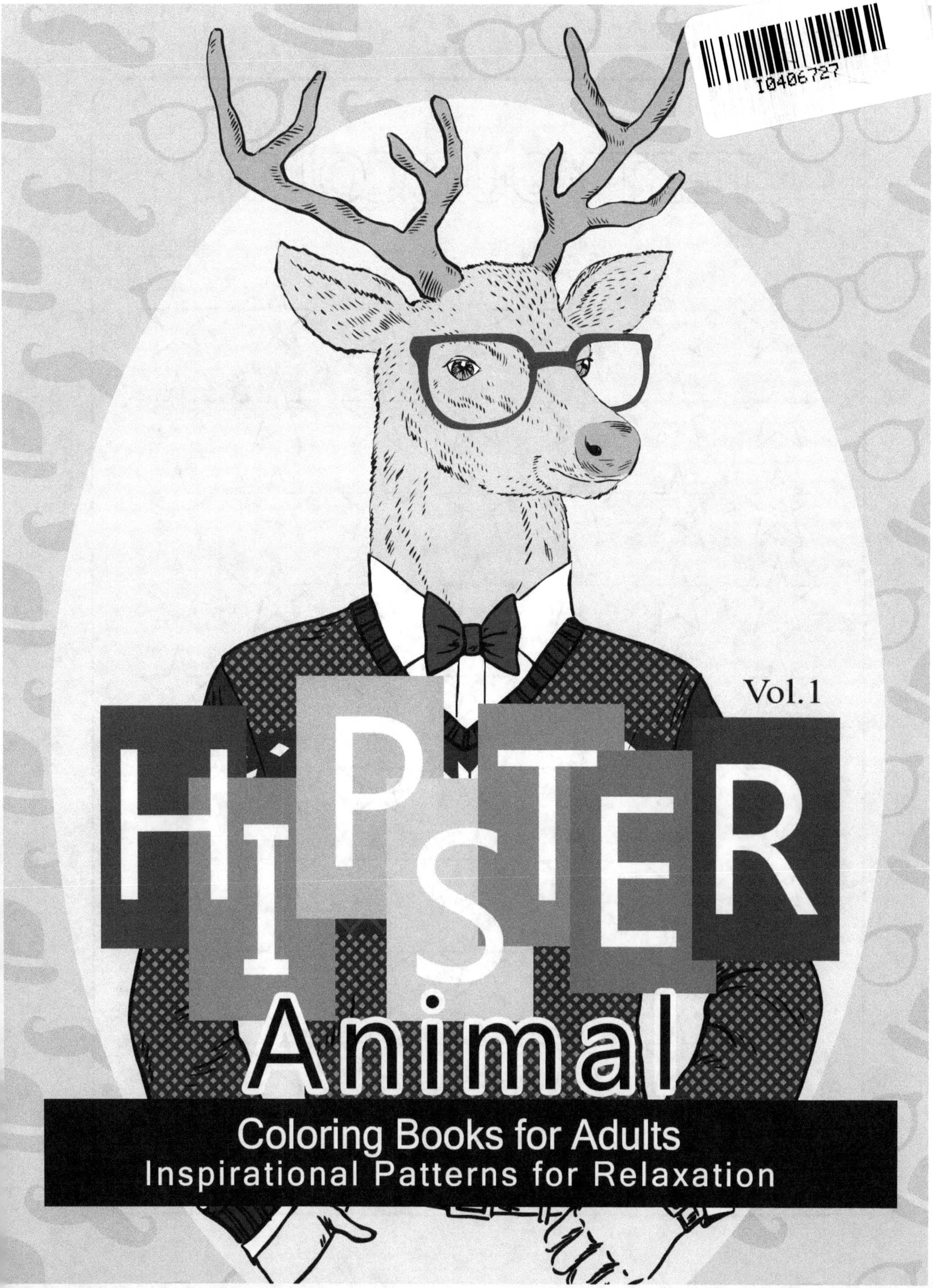
Vol.1
HIPSTER
Animal
Coloring Books for Adults
Inspirational Patterns for Relaxation

TEST YOUR COLOR

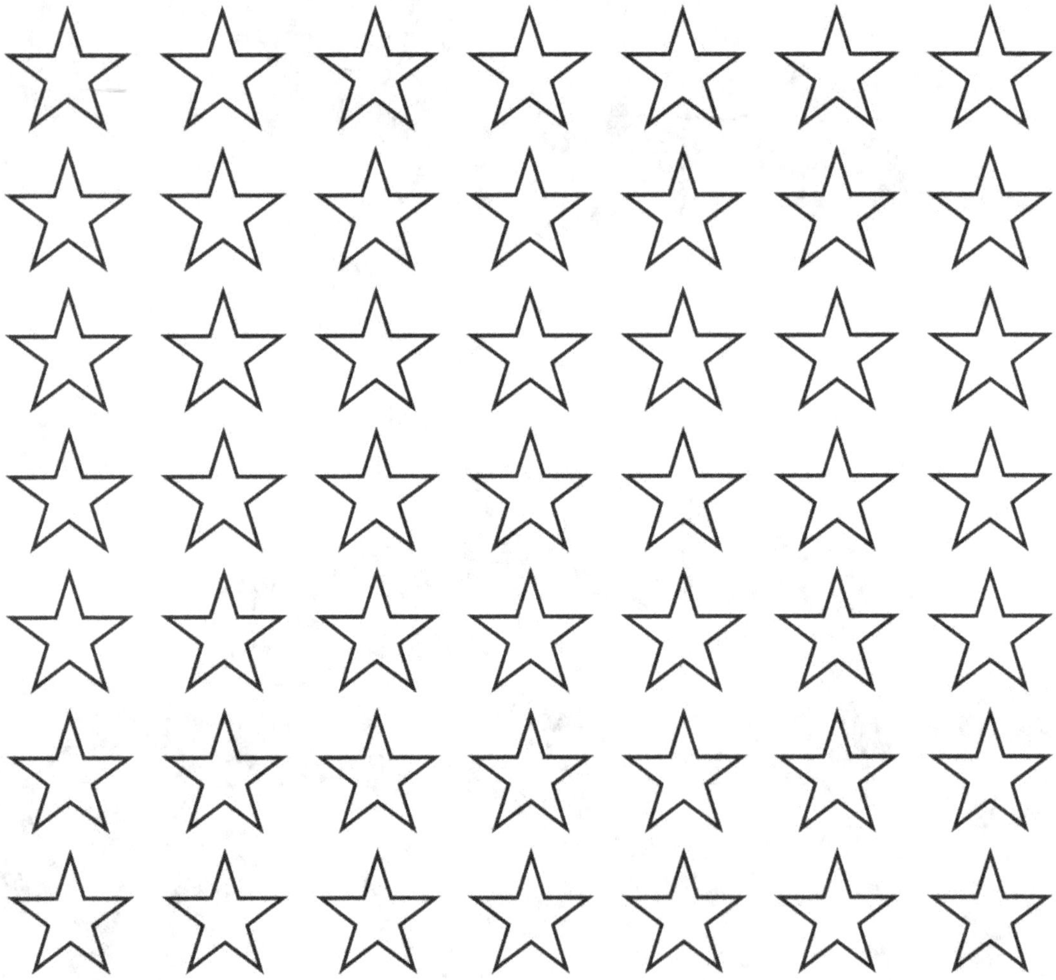

TEST YOUR COLOR

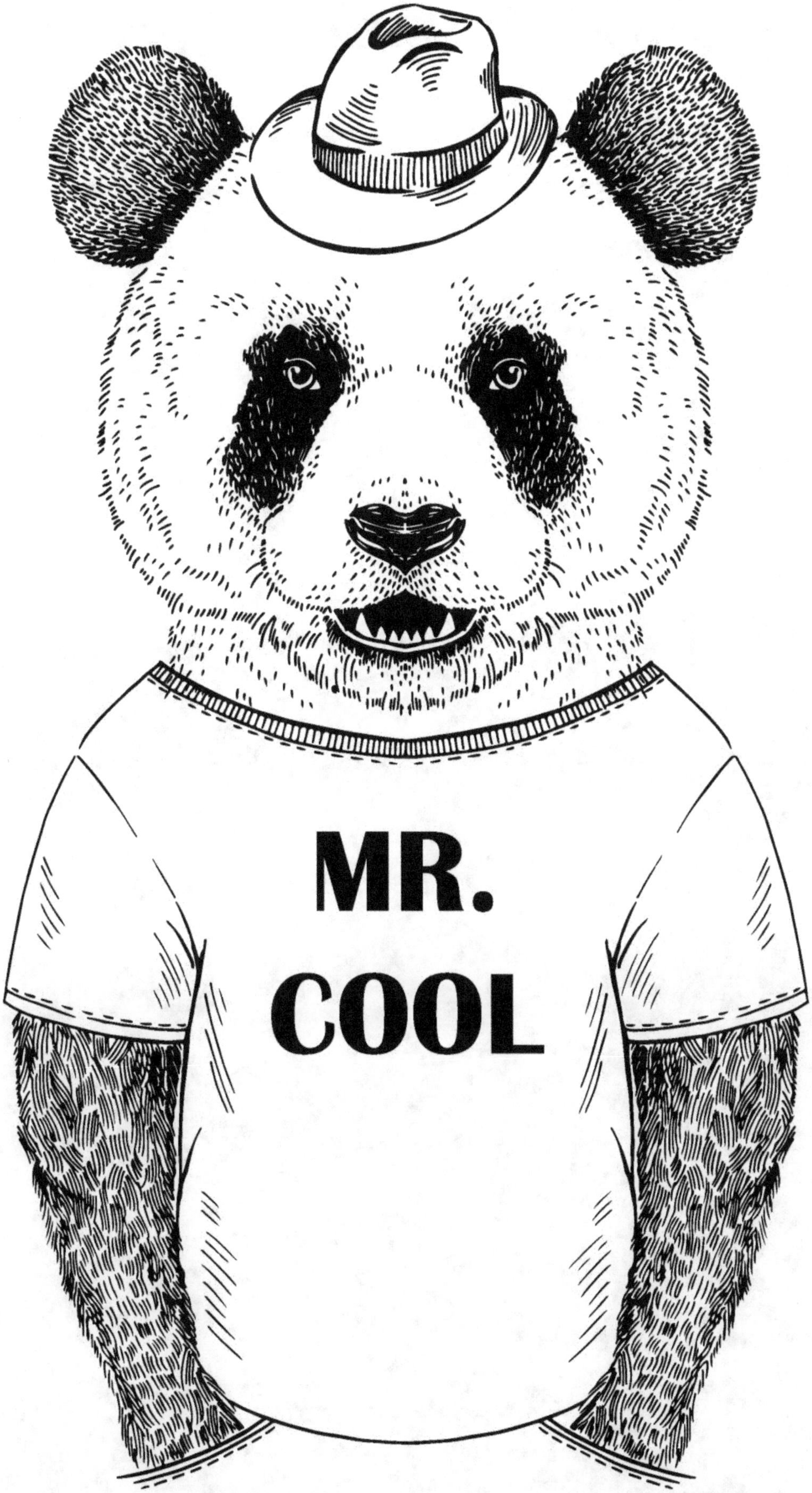
MR.
COOL

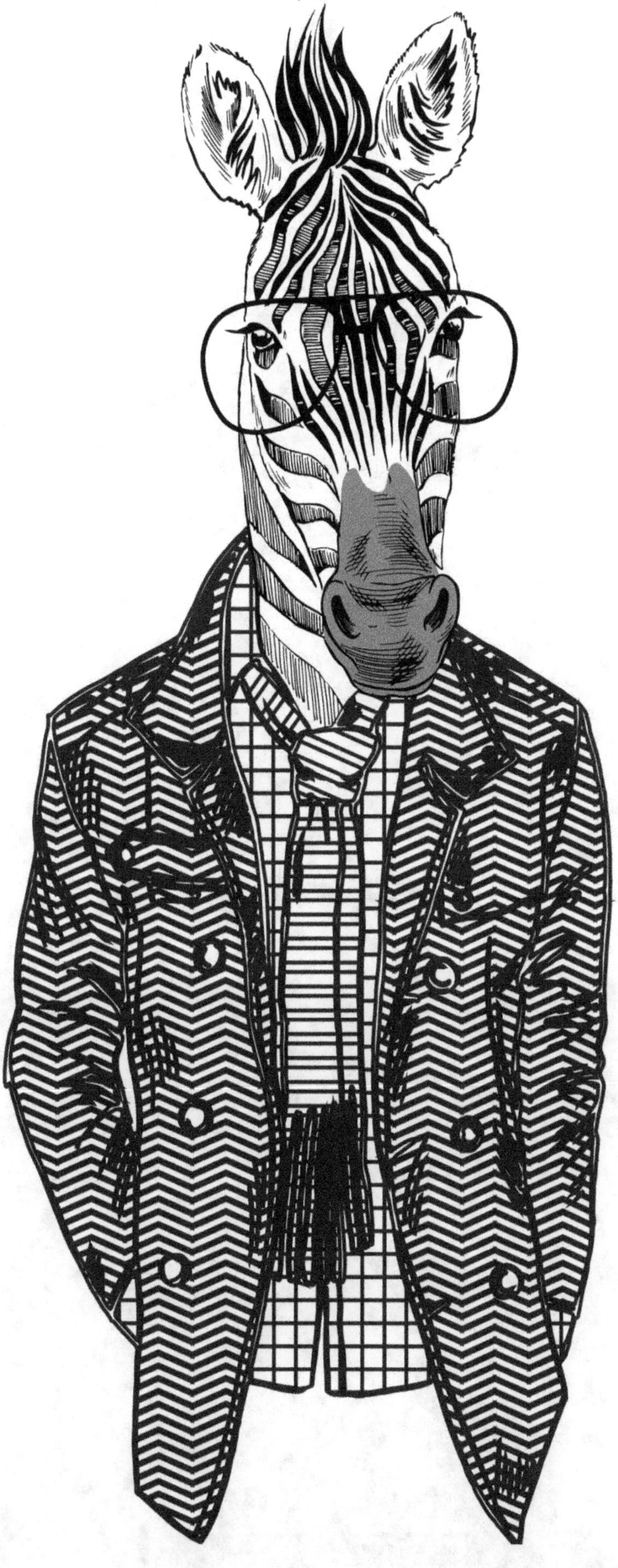

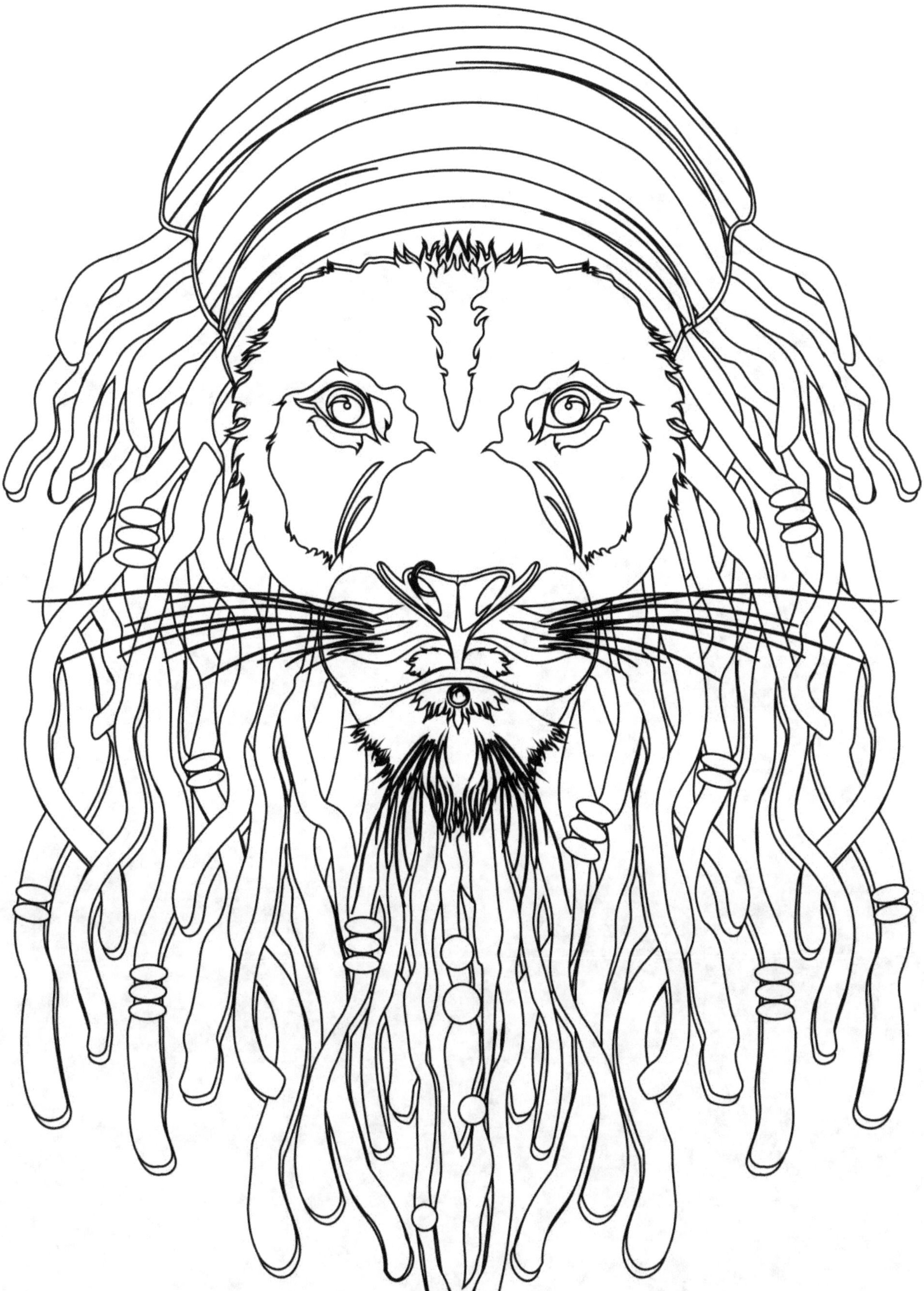

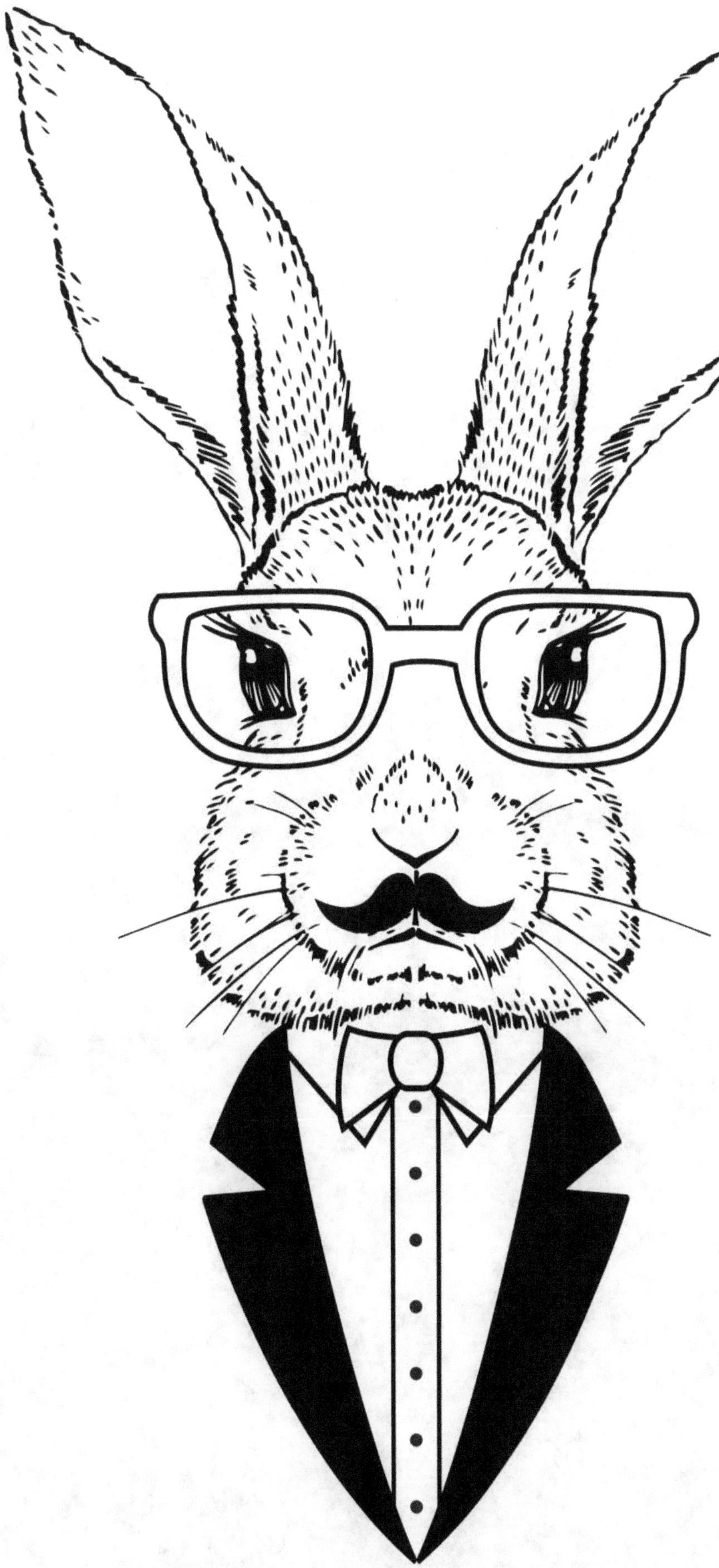

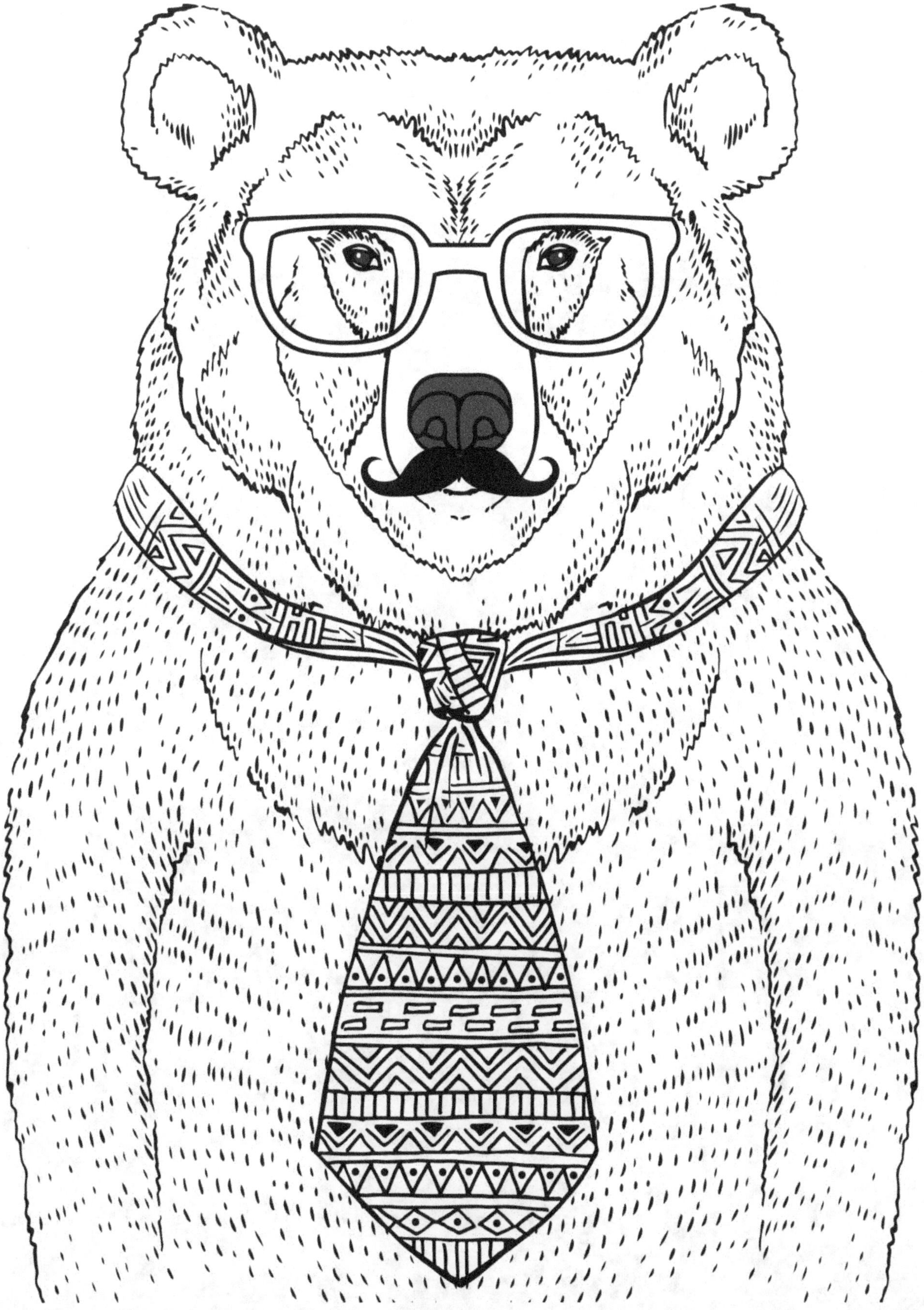

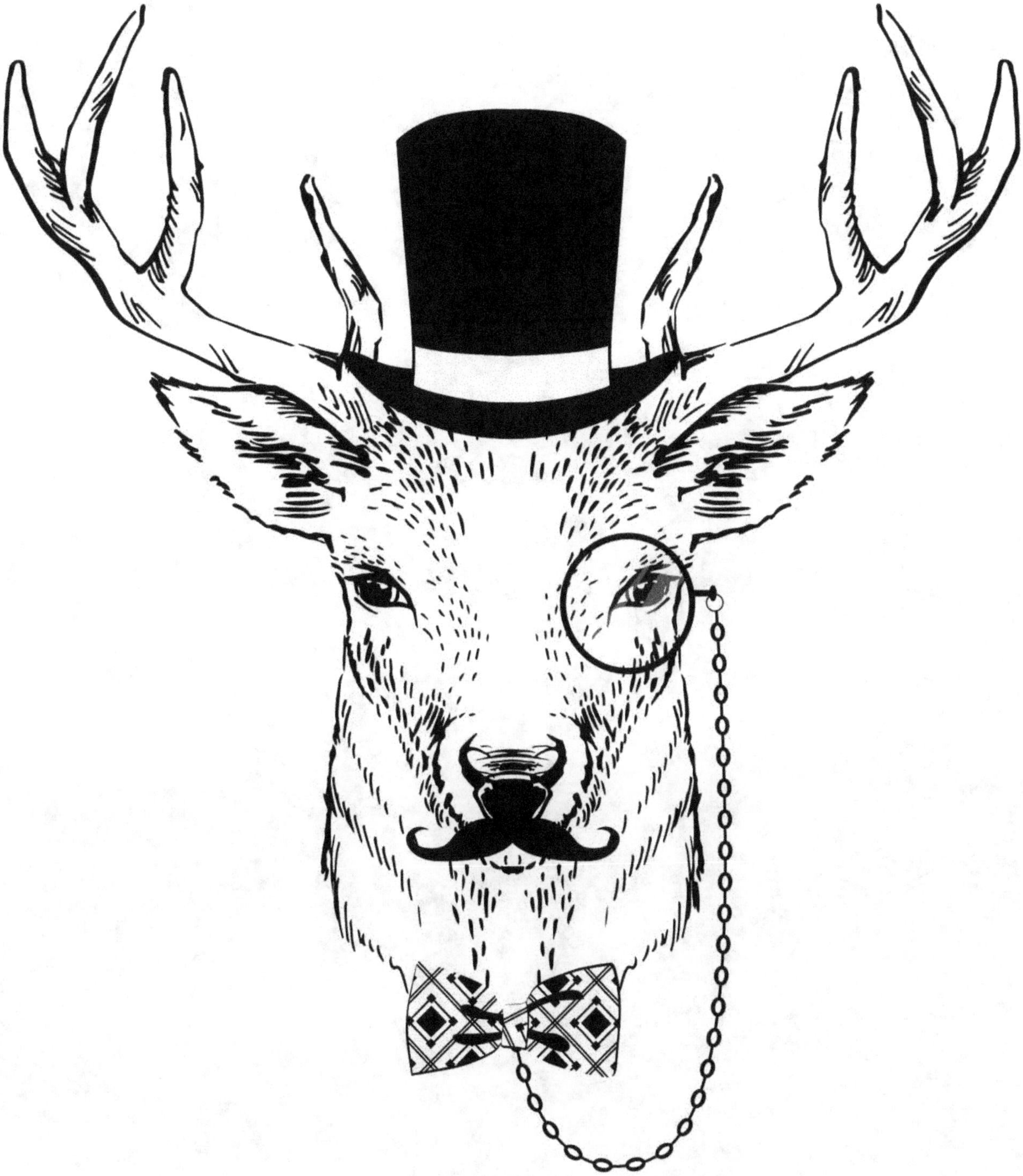

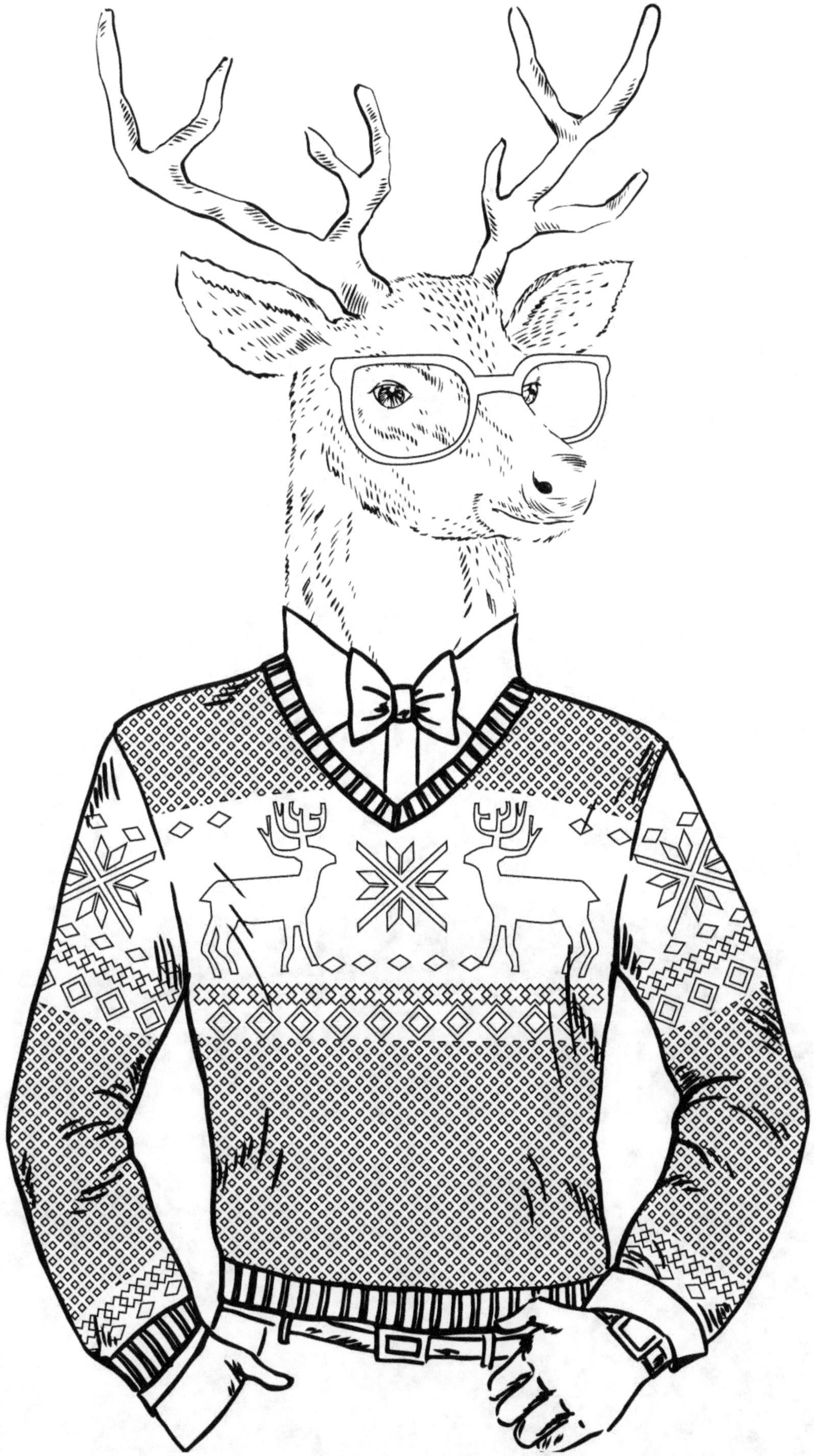

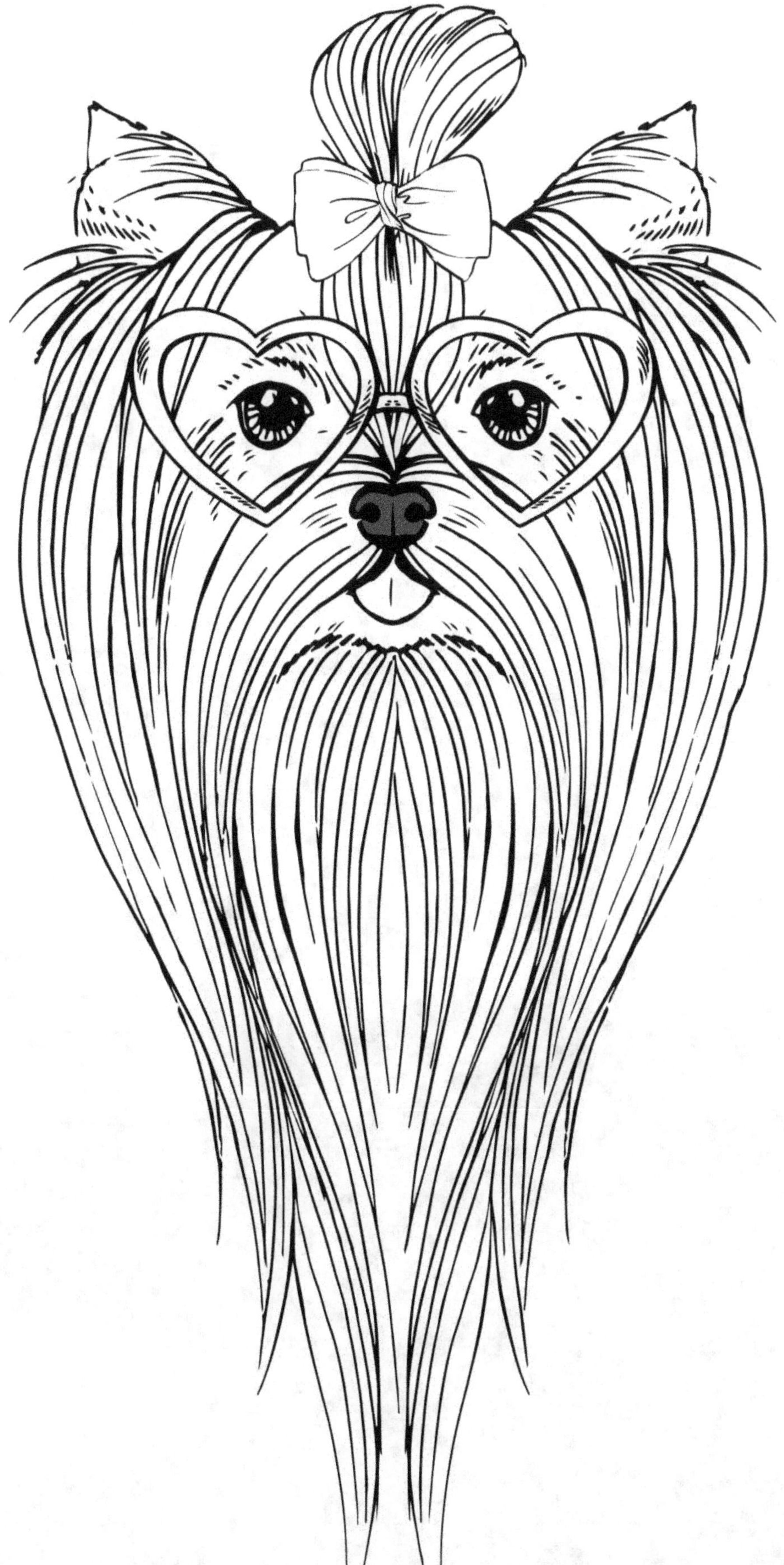

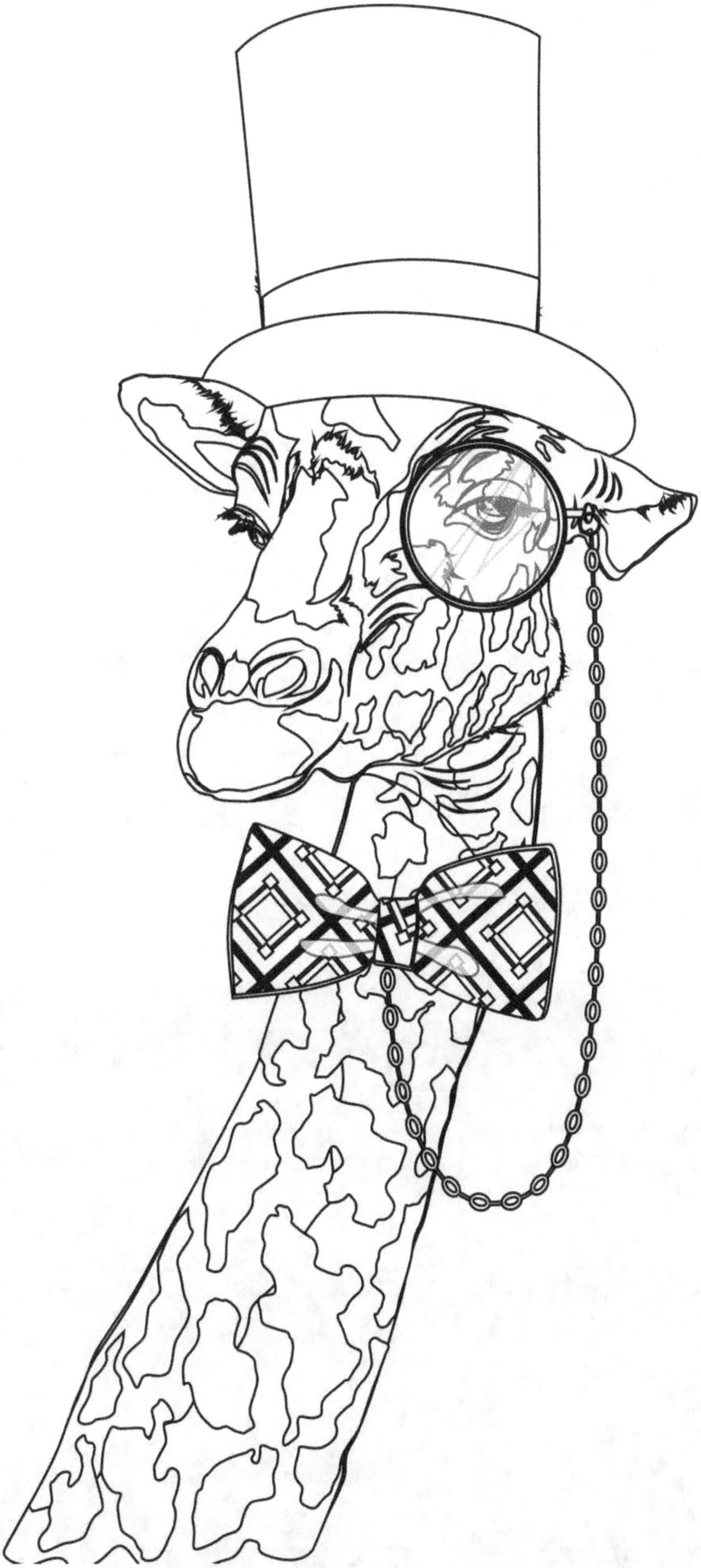

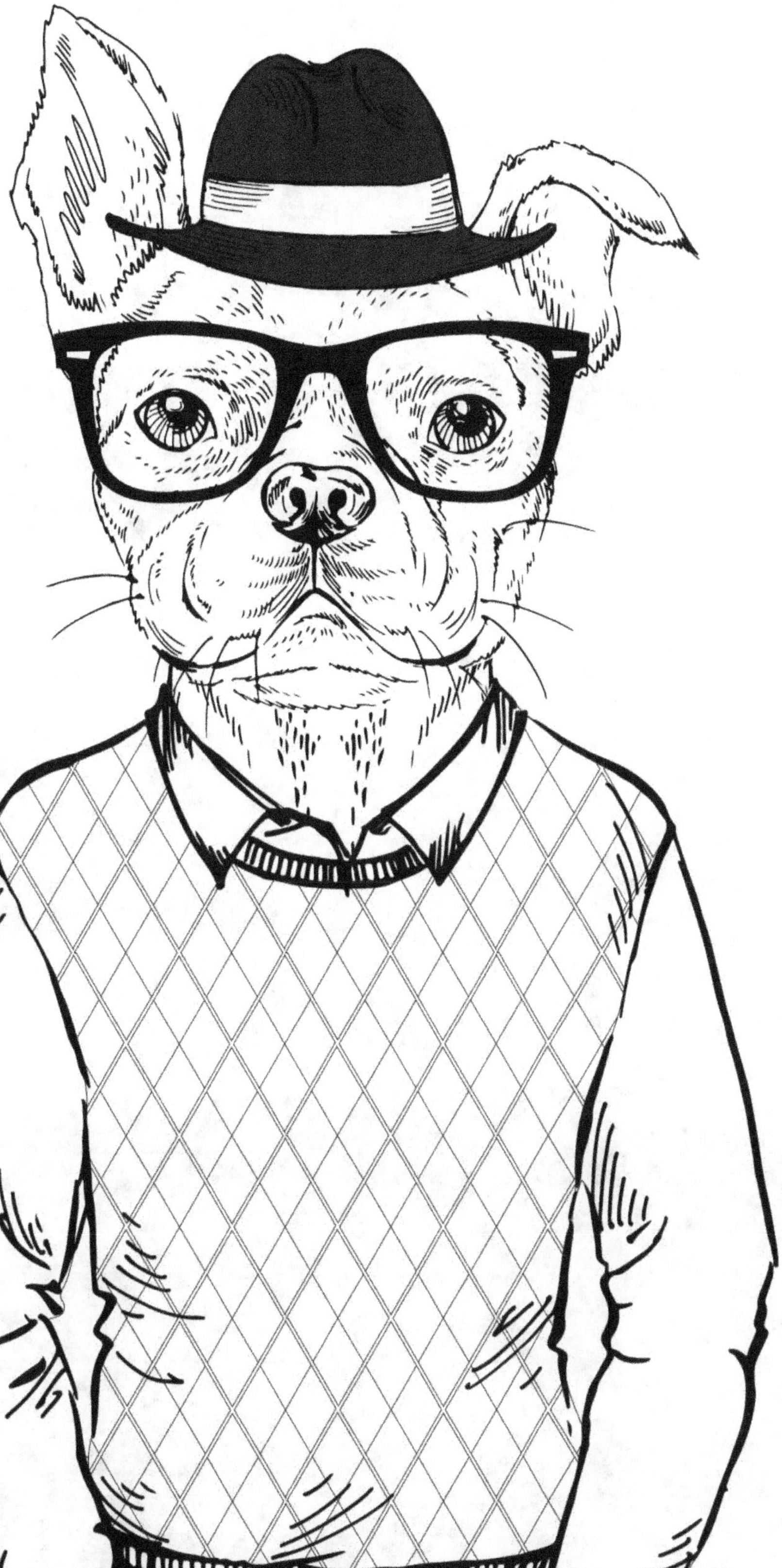

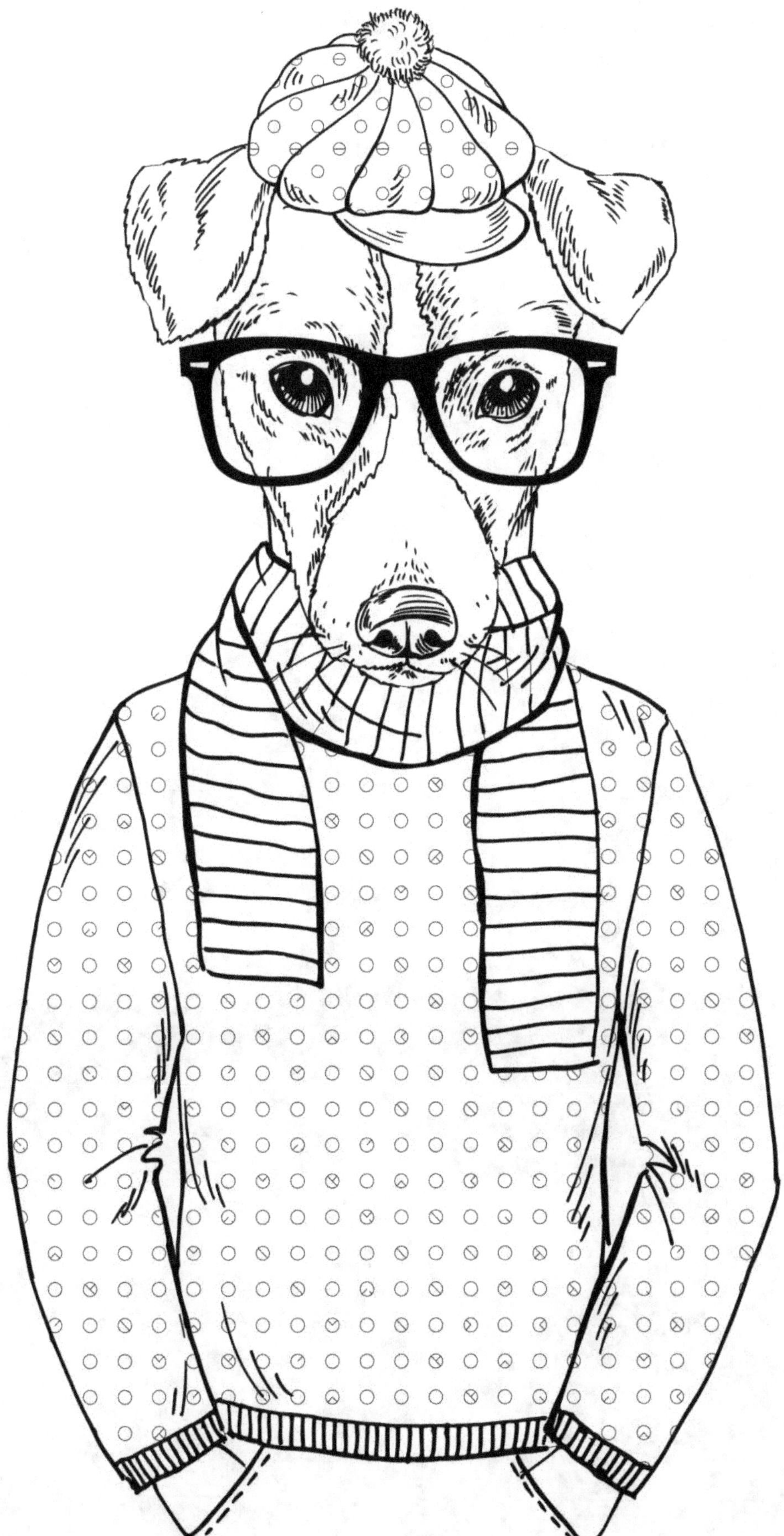

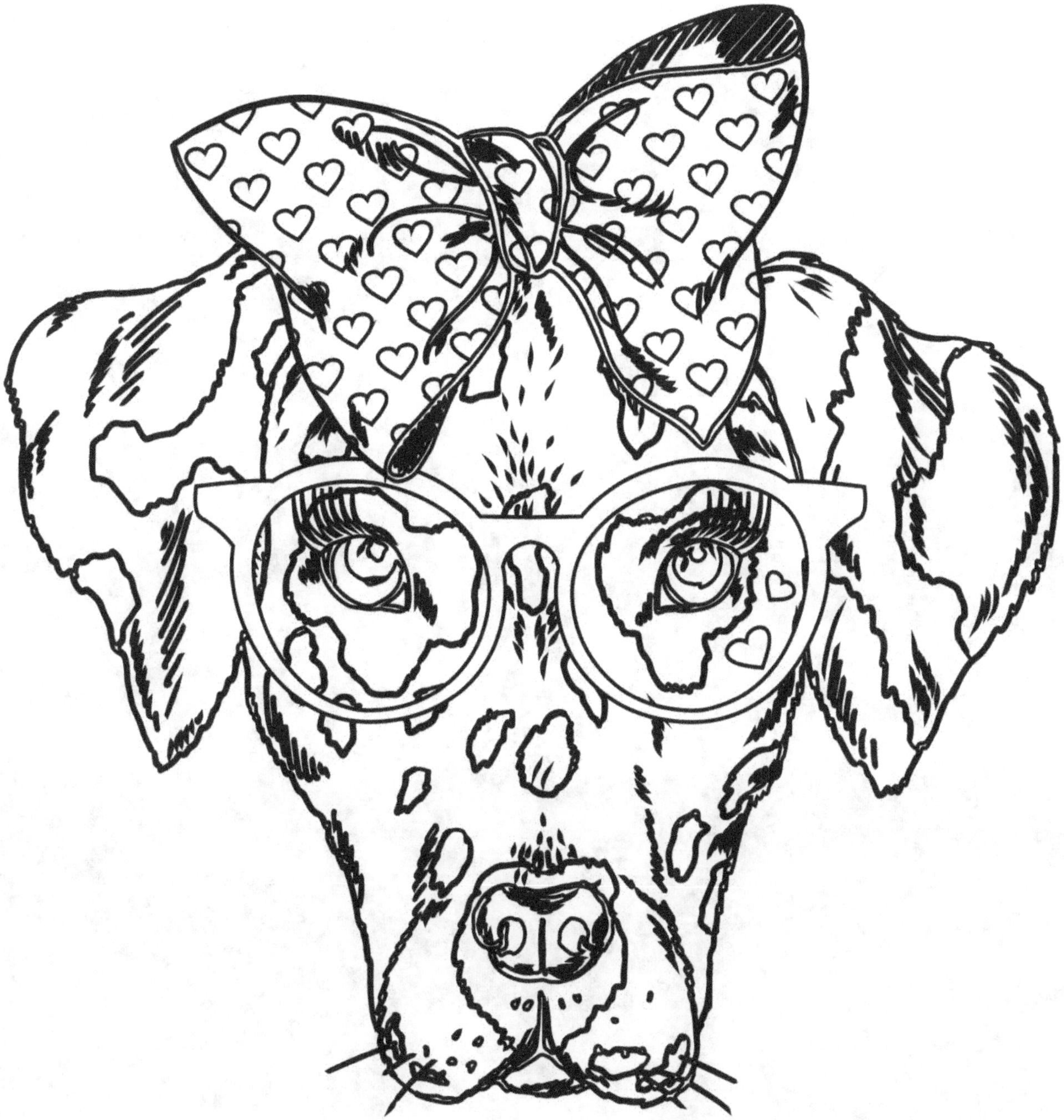

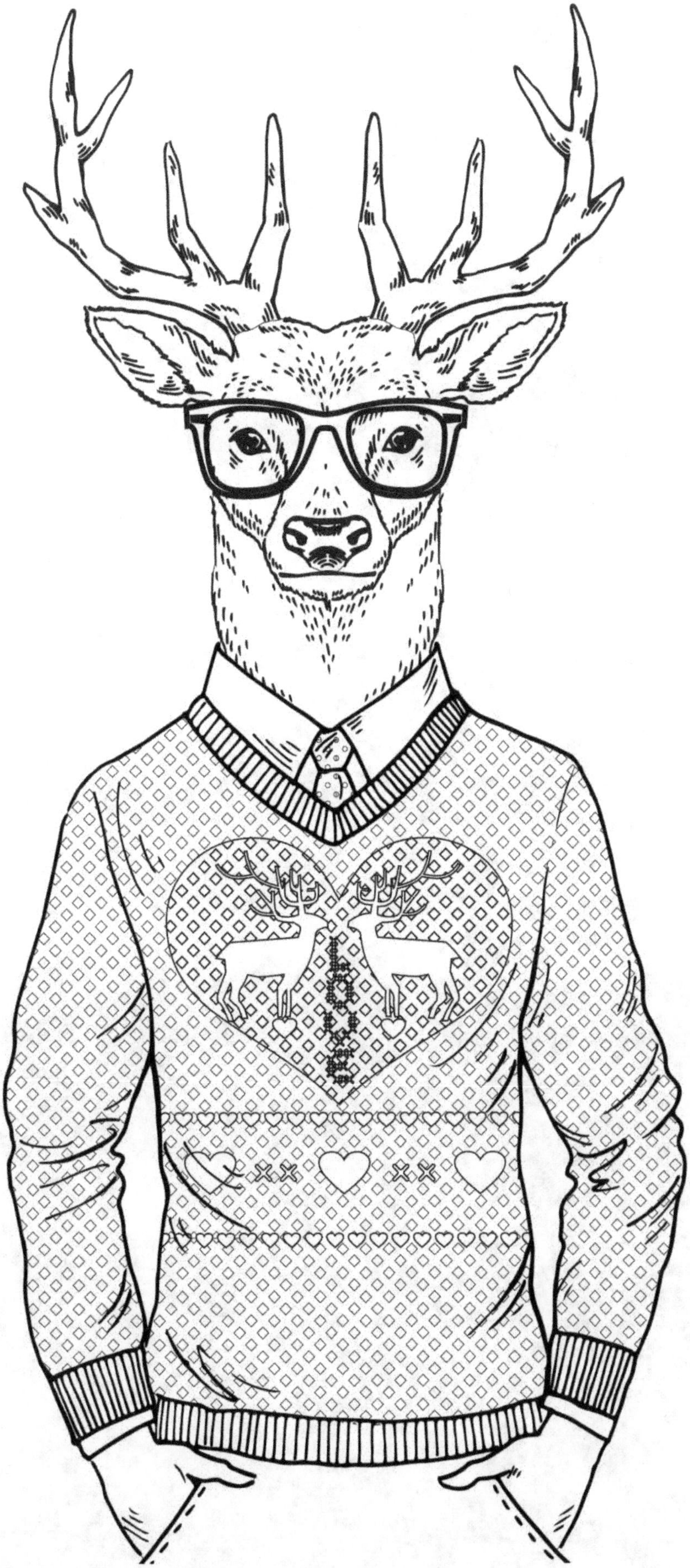

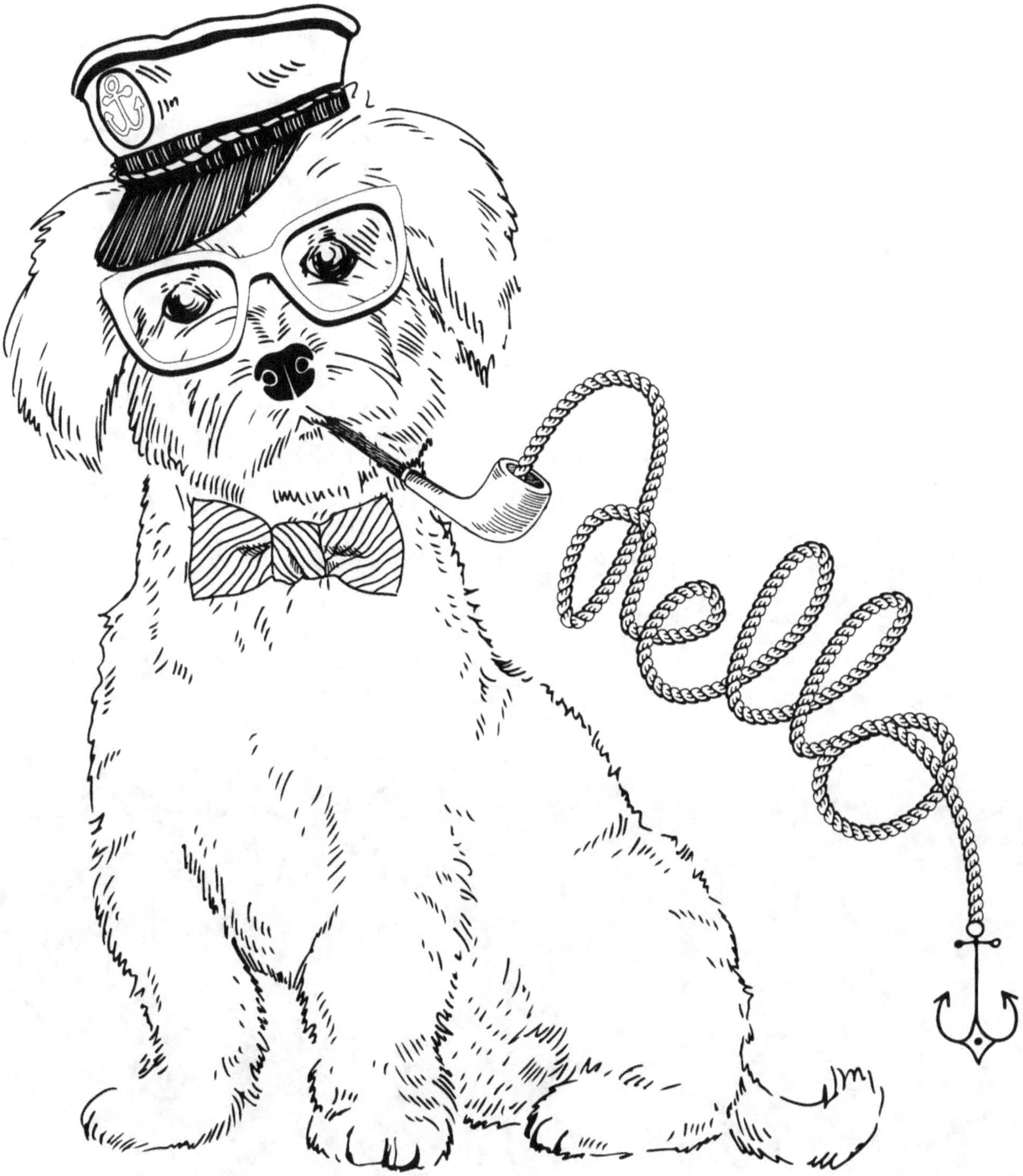
hello

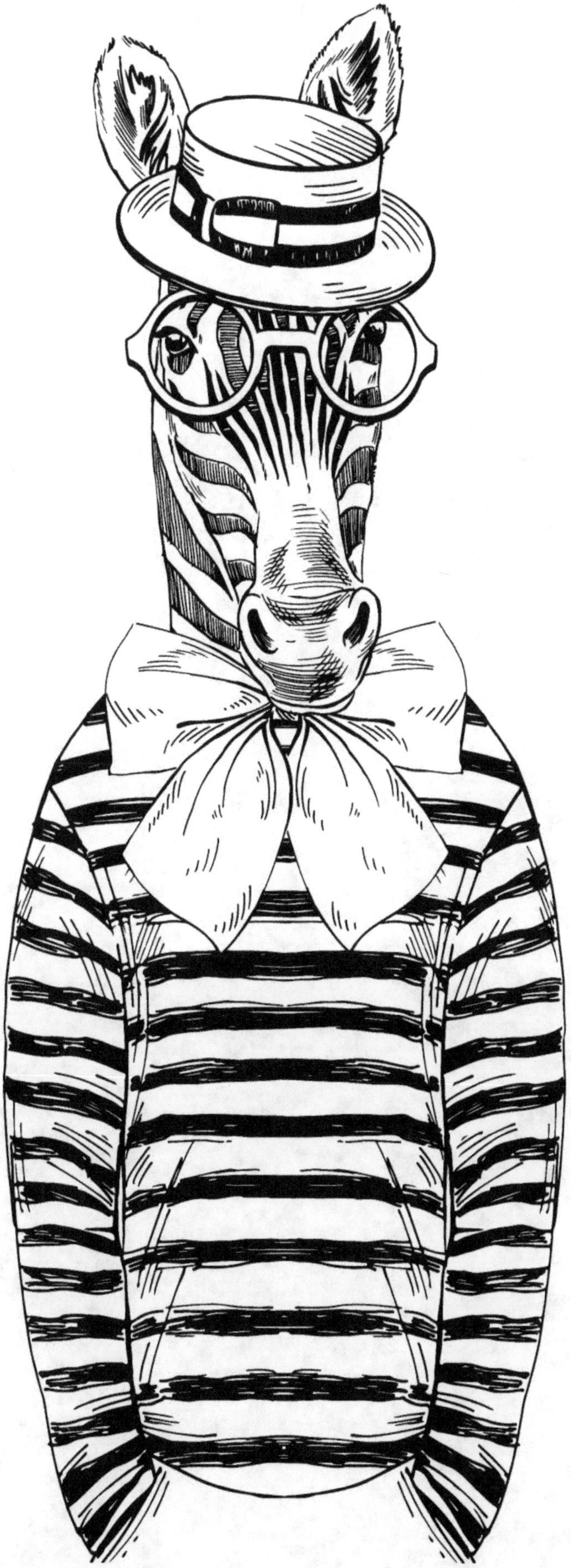

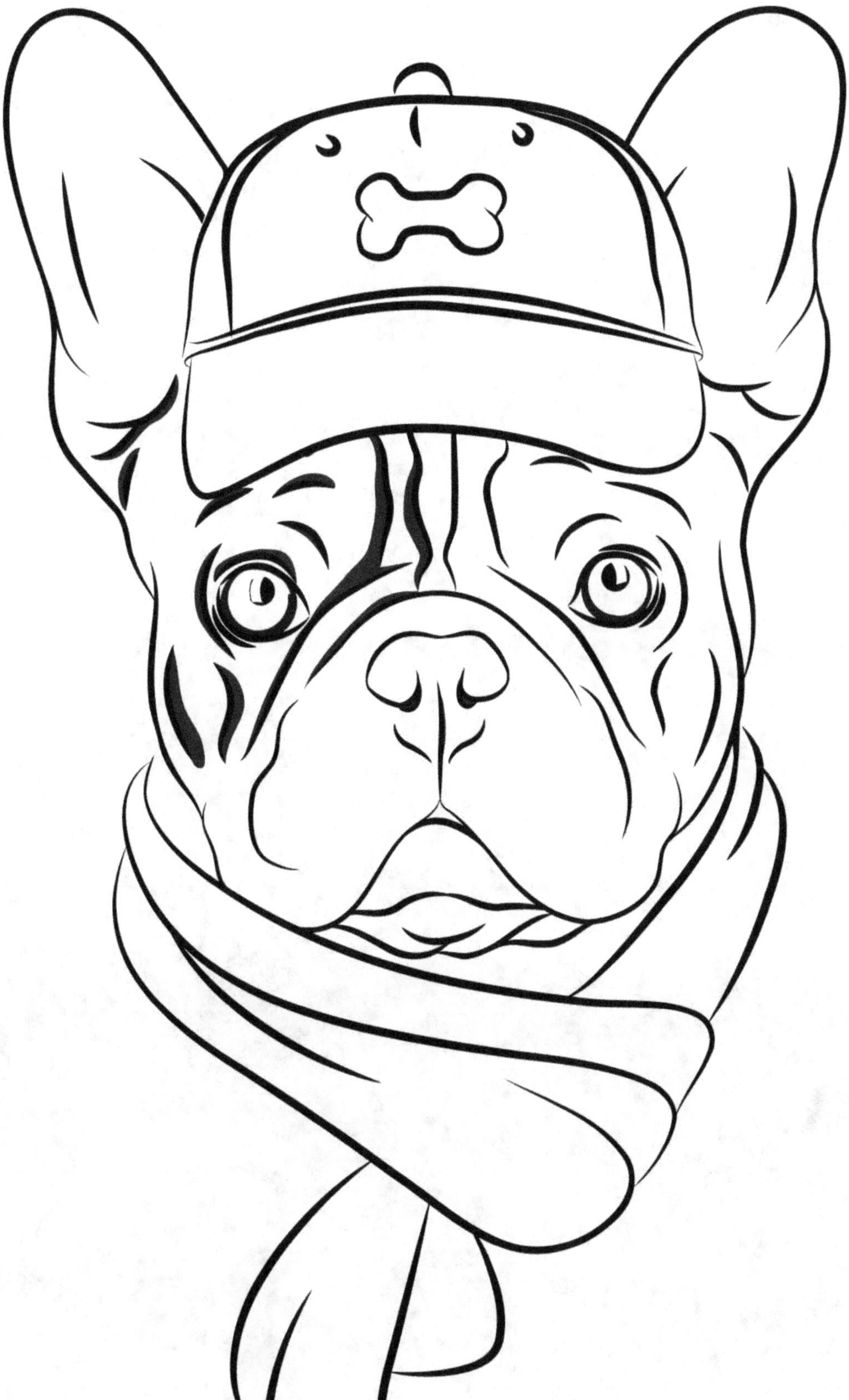

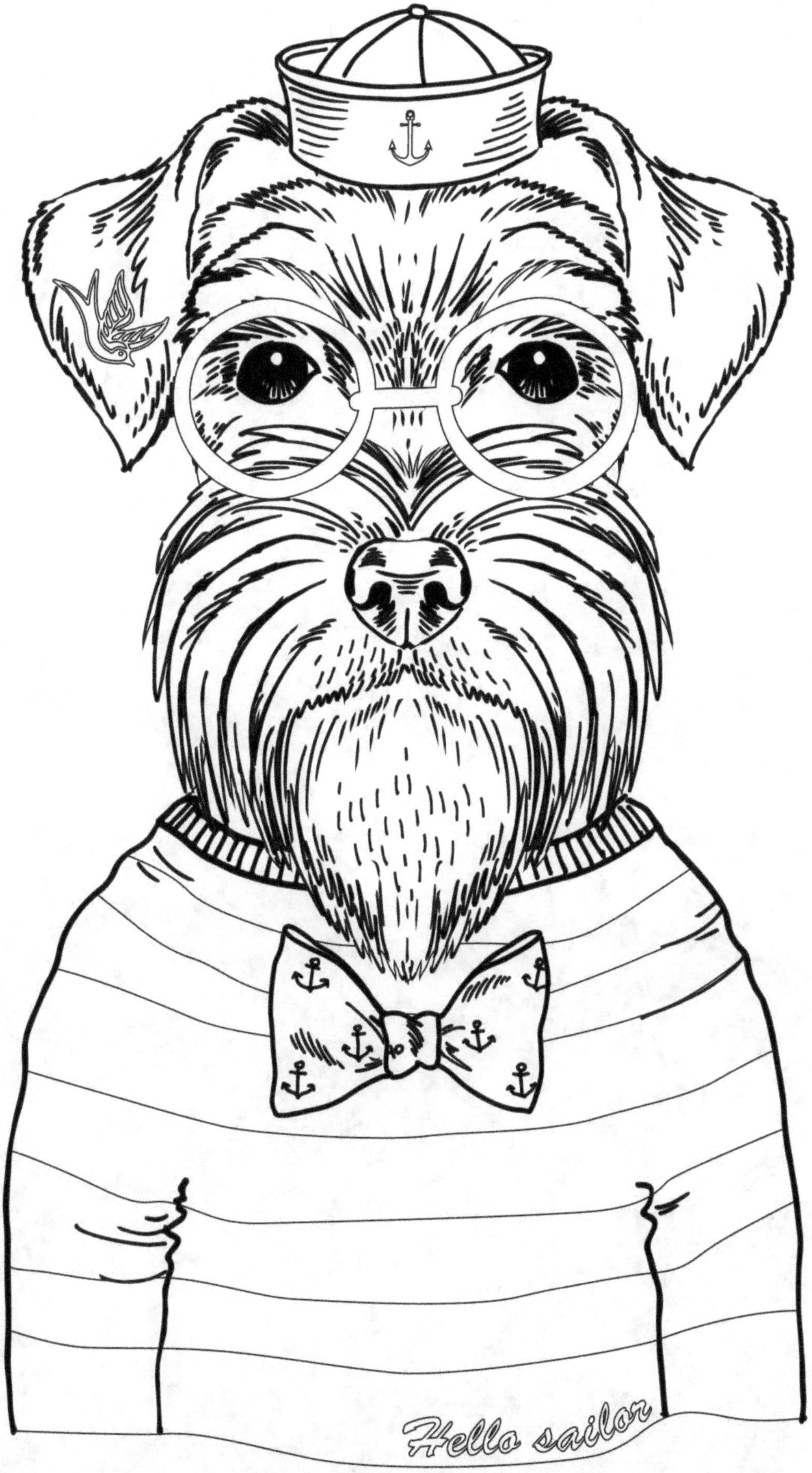
Hello sailor

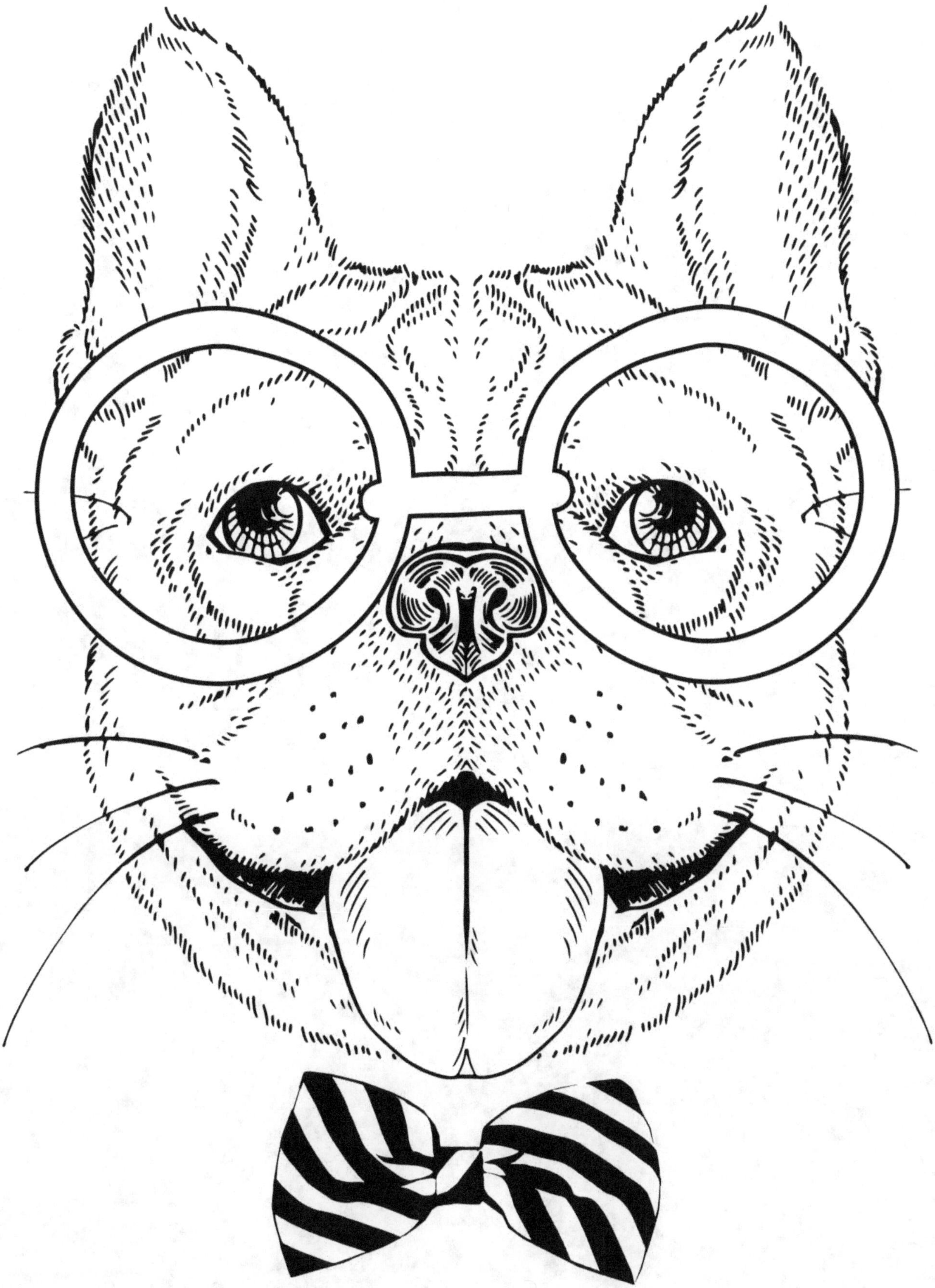

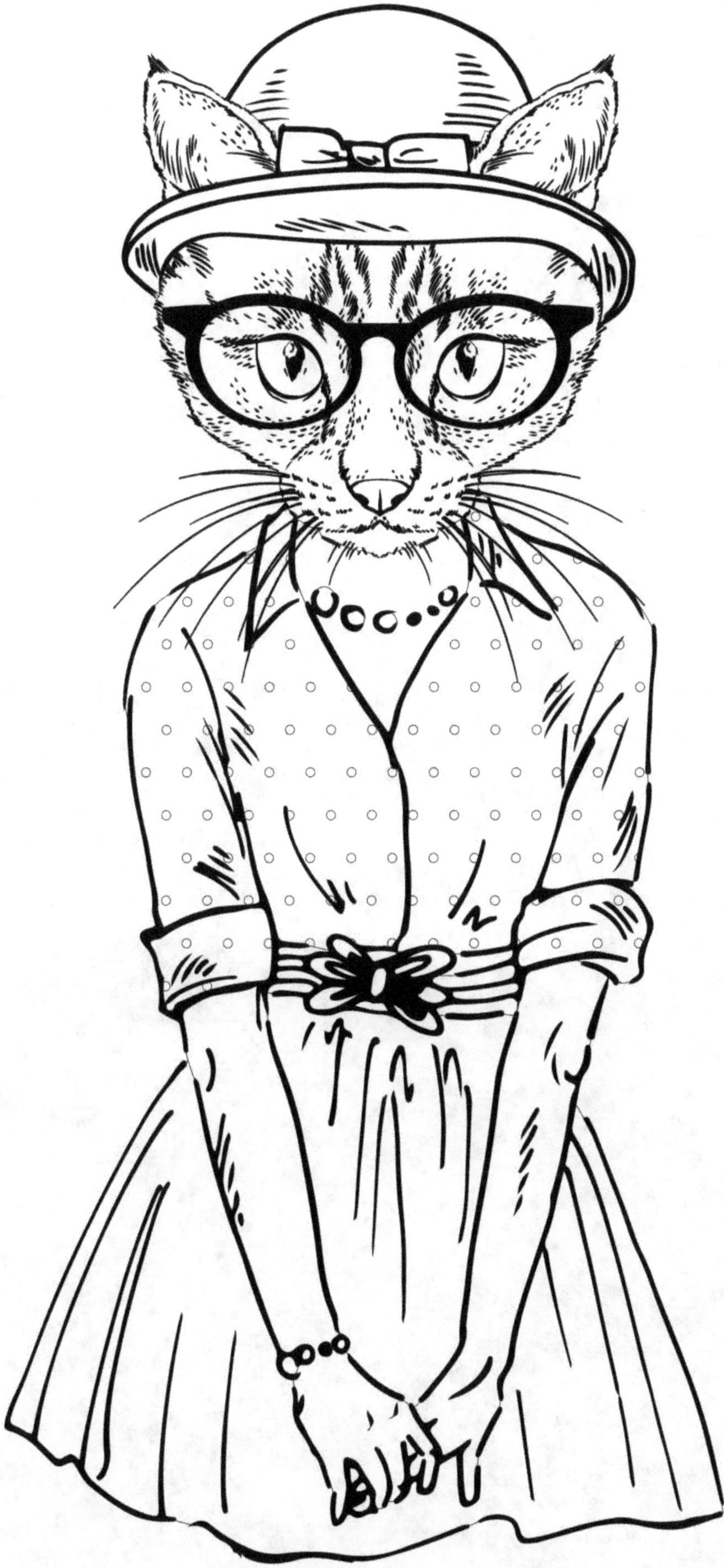

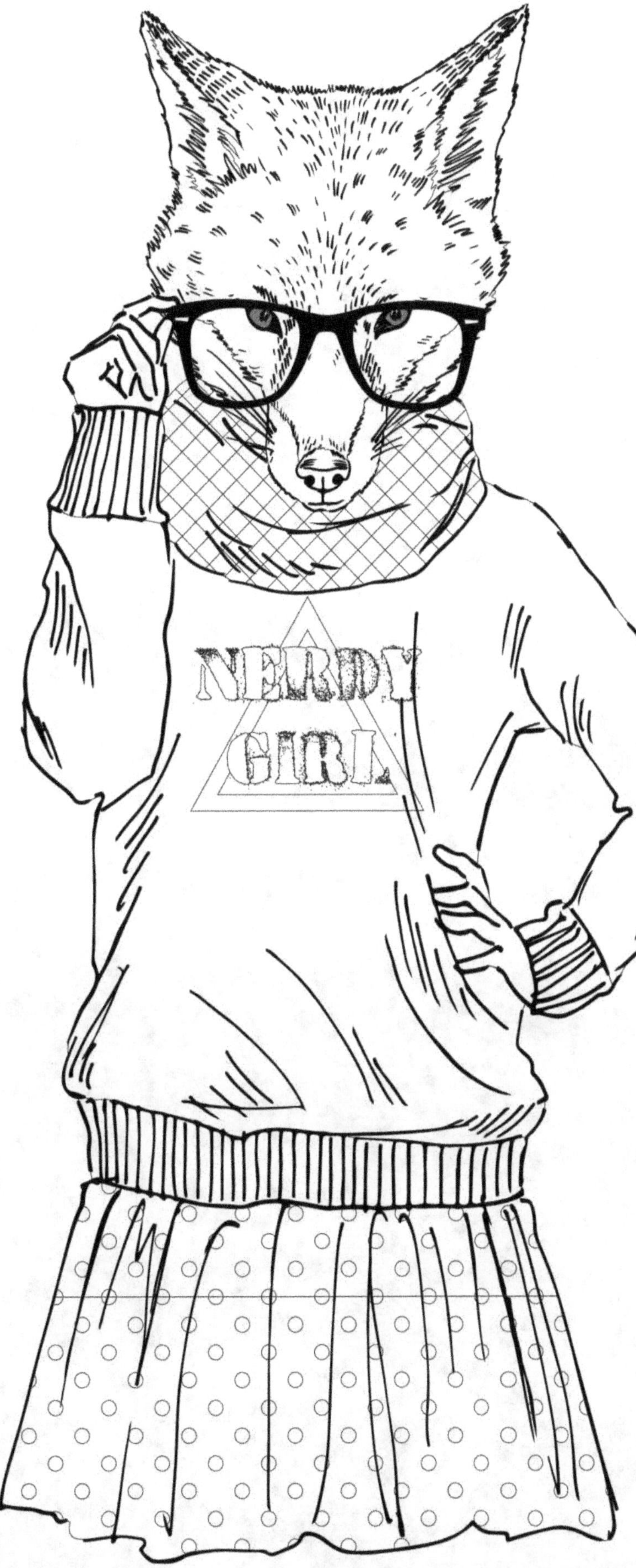
NERDY
GIRL

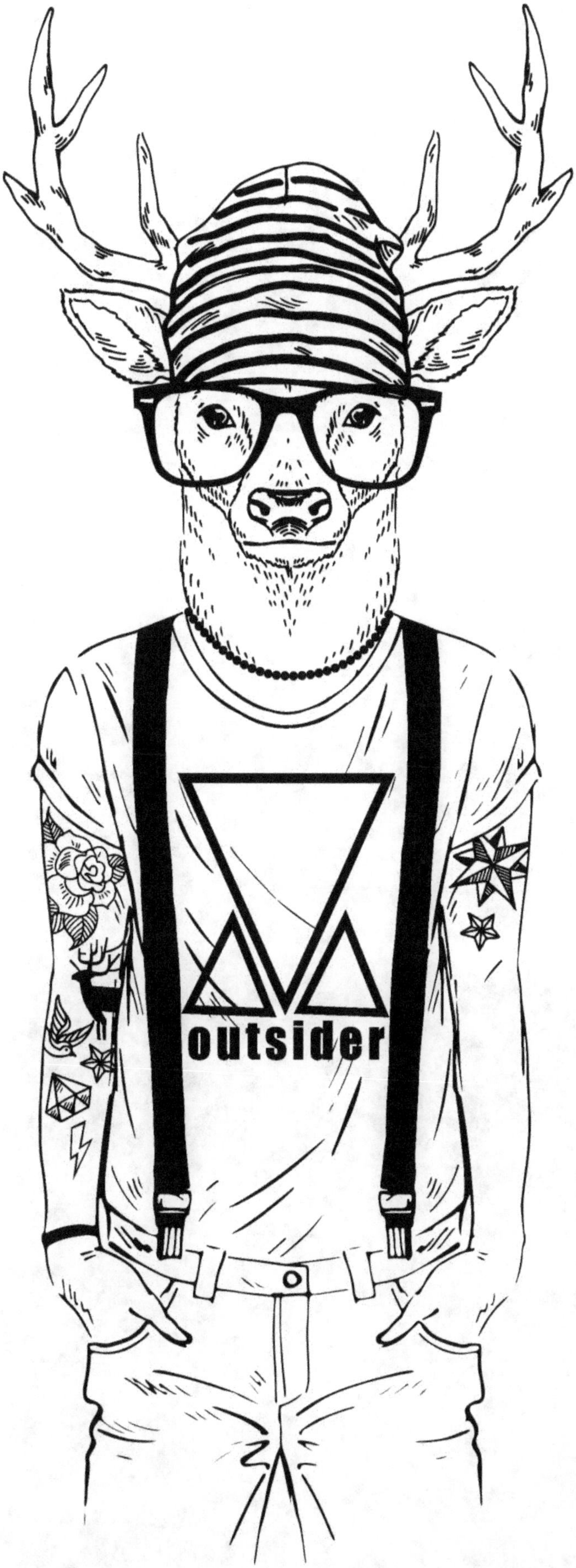
outsider

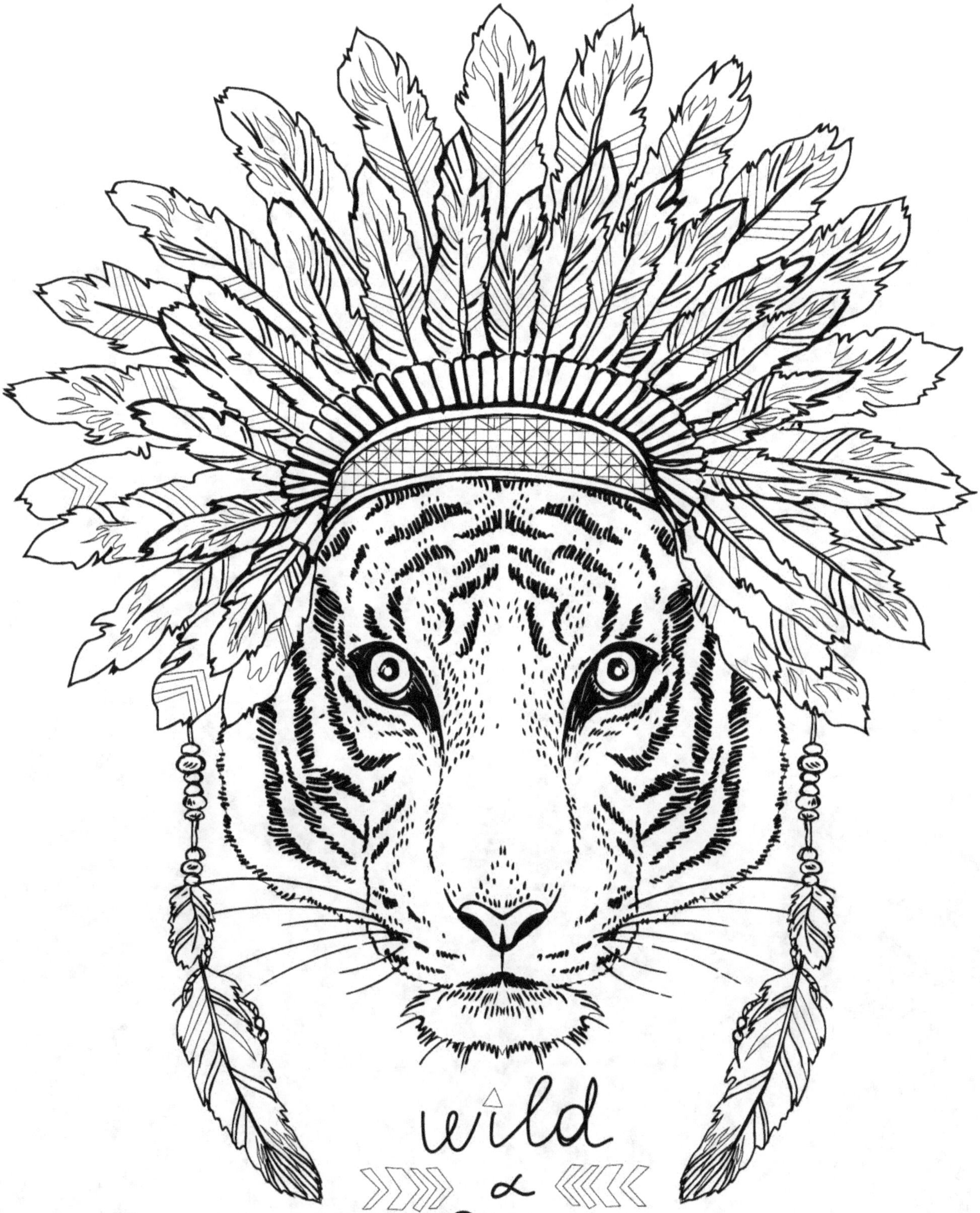
wild
&
free...

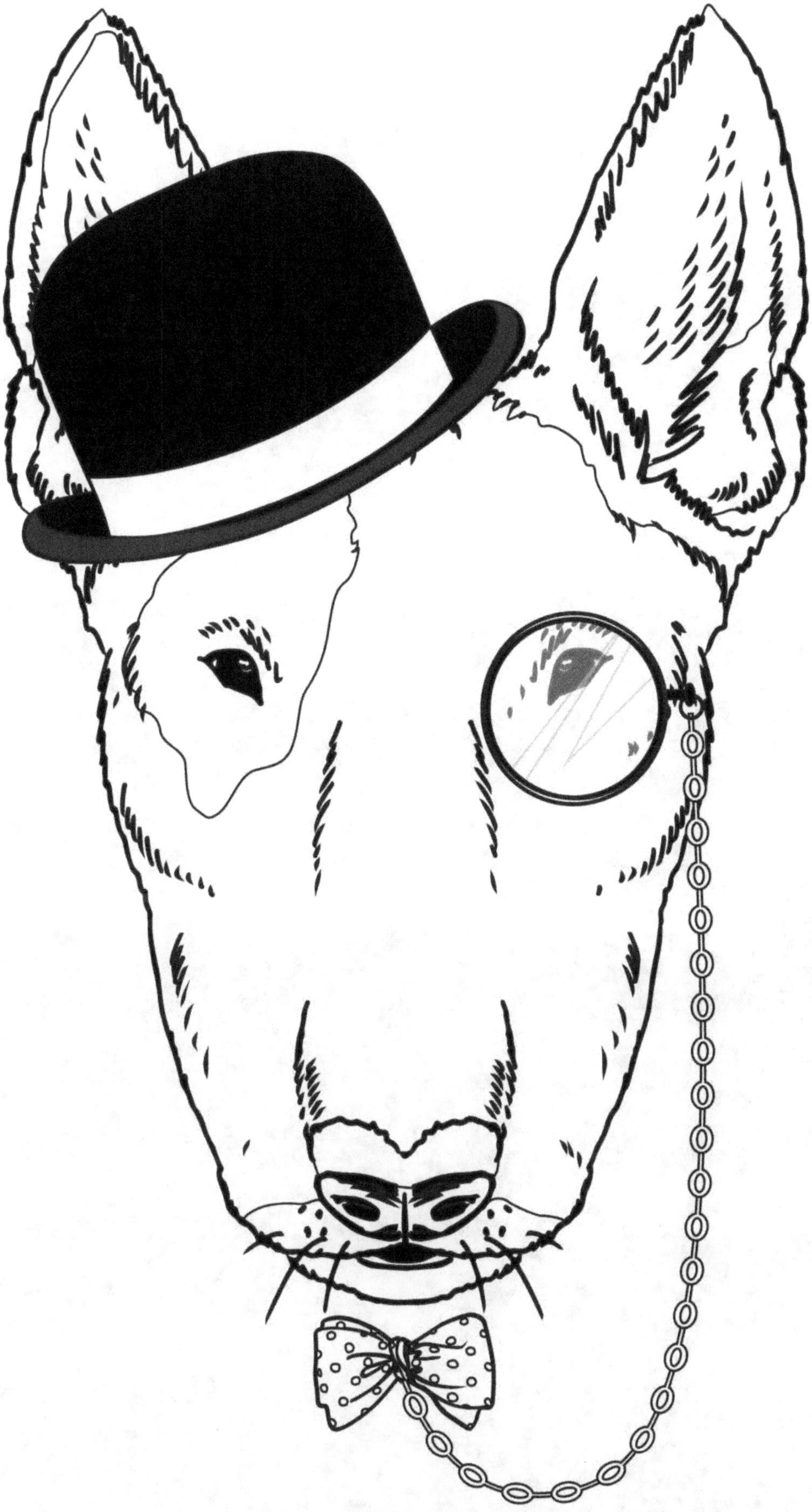

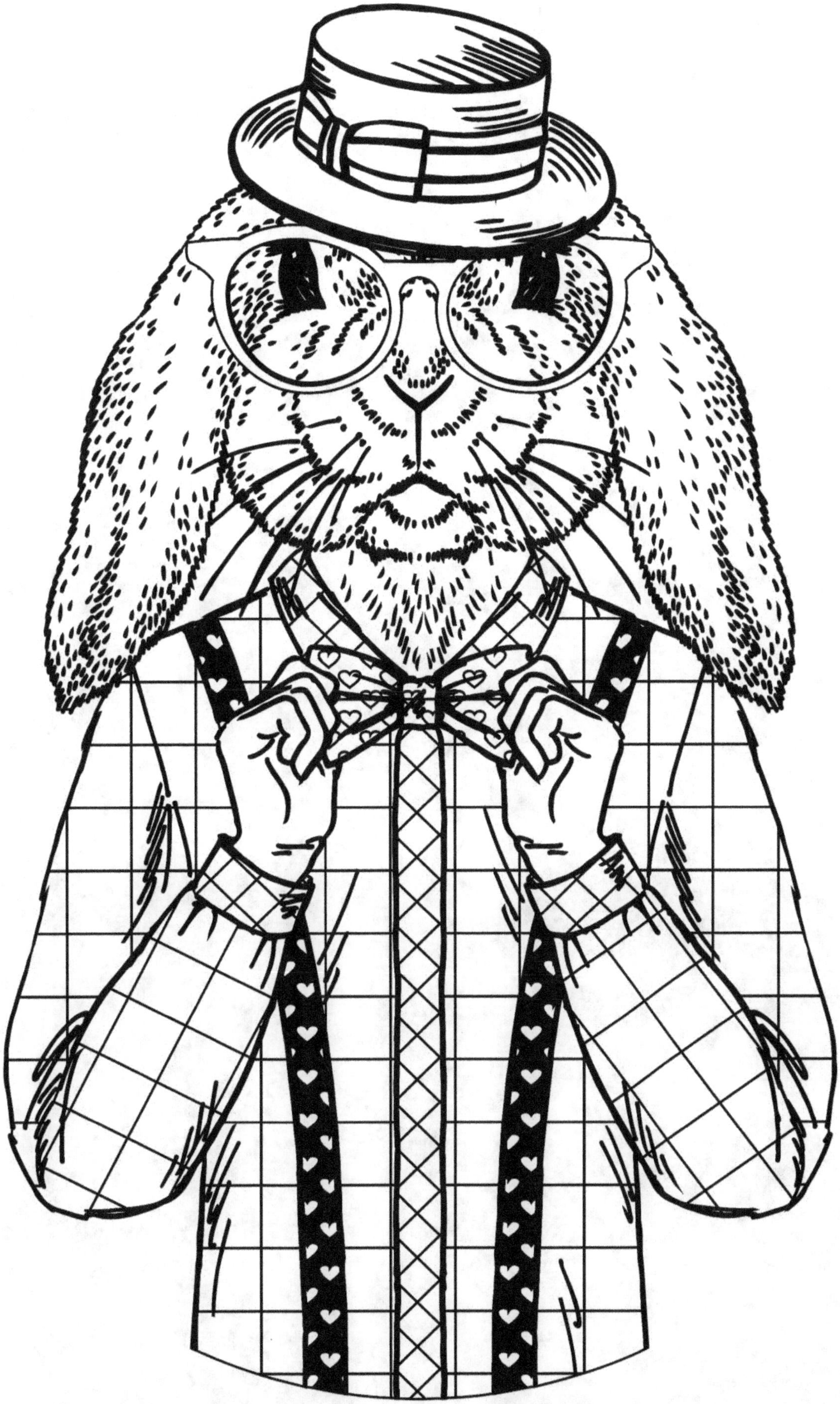

www.ingramcontent.com/pod-product-compliance
Lightning Source LLC
Chambersburg PA
CBHW081305180526
45170CB00007B/2578
9781541274884